Celebrate Thanksgiving!

Jay J. Harris

MEDIA BOOKS

New York

Celebrate Thanksgiving!

© by Media Books

First paperback edition 1988

Acknowledgments: Recipes selected and organized by Phyllis Gabrielle Supplice. Other assistance or information supplied by the Jamestown-Yorktown Foundation, Old Sturbridge Village, Plimoth Plantation, Plymouth County Development Council.

Library of Congress Cataloging-in-Publication Data
Harris, Jay, 1922-

1. Thanksgiving   I. Title.
GT4975.H37   1988   394.2'683   88-10434

ISBN 0-912064-04-8

Printed in the United States of America

Distributed by Alpha Book Distributors,
303 West 10 Street, New York, NY 10014-2599; tel. 212/675-8749; 800/221-8112

To Phyllis... and to those Americans who may recall learning something about our Pilgrim forefathers but are a bit fuzzy on the details.

Contents

Preface

For well over a century, Thanksgiving has been an annual national observance. The origin and significance of any celebration can easily become obscured over such a long period. So, while Thanksgiving Dinners bring families and friends together all over our country, the richness of the holiday's history is often ignored.

A feature of "Celebrate Thanksgiving!" is a section devoted to the history of the holiday and its traditional dinner. This section is prepared in a format planned so all who are joined for the festivities can participate in a ceremony celebrating the occasion.

"Celebrate Thanksgiving!" can help you make your feast more meaningful and truly memorable for all.

The "Celebrate Thanksgiving!" Celebration

Introduction

Everyone at your Thanksgiving Day Dinner can join in to find out more about the origins and significance of the holiday and its observance.

It is suggested that this section be read aloud by members of the dinner party before dinner is served. You may find it best to set aside an adequate period of time well before the meal preparation is completed. If preparations are well advanced, the host or hostess, or both, will enjoy taking the role designated as "leader" of the ceremony. If this is not convenient, they can designate another to read their part. The leader calls upon others by name to read the "participant" sections.

> The host or hostess may wish to improvise, or add to the text. For example, it might be appropriate to mention near the end of the ceremony those events or other matters for which the family is particularly thankful.

> Large type has been used in this section so children can easily take part. Their participation will certainly enhance their appreciation of the holiday and its role in American history.

> The celebration will be much easier to conduct if each participant has his or her own text to follow and read. A personal copy of the complete "Celebrate Thanksgiving!" to keep would serve as a fine momento of the event. However, you may prefer to photocopy this section with sufficient copies for your group. For this purpose, the publisher waives the restrictions against reproduction of this section—but for private use only by those participants at your dinner.

If there are more at the dinner than there are "Participant" sections, parts of the "I Didn't Know *That* About Thanksgiving" chapter may be read aloud so everyone has a speaking role in the celebration.

(Note: Various historical accounts about the Pilgrims differ on a number of aspects. The information used here is based on generally-accepted and, to the extent possible, verified historical reports.)

Enjoy your special "Celebrate Thanksgiving!" Dinner!

The Celebration

Leader:

We're gathered together today to enjoy a special dinner. It's special because it's an American Thanksgiving Dinner. It's part of a tradition that goes back many years. Let's find out why we celebrate Thanksgiving. Who started the tradition?

Participant:

Over three hundred and fifty years ago, a group of people who became known as Pilgrims lived in England. They left their homes in that country because the English king would not let them worship God in the way they wanted. They knew the king would put them in prison if they disobeyed his orders.

Leader:

Where did the Pilgrims go when they left their homes in England?

Participant:

They went to Holland and lived there for over ten years. But the Pilgrims became unhappy that their children were taking on more of the Dutch ways. For this and other reasons they decided to move again. This time they planned to go to North America. It would take great courage to set out on a voyage to the New World. Little was known about America then. To the Pilgrims, it would have seemed like going to another planet.

They were aware that it would take many weeks to cross the Atlantic Ocean. They knew too that heavy waves might pound their ship. The land they would reach if all went well was mostly covered by forests. It was the home of Native Americans, who were then called Indians, and many of them did not like new people invading their land. But the Pilgrims were determined to move to the New World.

Leader:

How did the Pilgrims get to America?

Participant:

Their friends in England helped them get two sailing ships. One was called Speedwell. It took the Pilgrims back to England but it leaked badly and couldn't be used for the ocean crossing. The other was a three-masted ship named the Mayflower. One hundred and two Pilgrims crowded aboard the Mayflower in the year 1620 to cross the Atlantic Ocean.

The winds blew hard and the seas were rough. As the days went by, the Pilgrims found they did not have enough fresh food on their ship. When the weather was bad, it was hard to prepare meals. The Pilgrims often went to bed hungry and cold.

The voyage took two months. By the time the Mayflower reached America, there was someone on board who had not started the trip. The new passenger was a baby boy, born on the ship to Elizabeth Hopkins. His mother named him Oceanus.

Leader:

Where did the Pilgrims land?

Participant:

The Pilgrims stepped ashore at what is now Provincetown on Cape Cod in the state of Massachusetts. William Bradford, who would later be re-elected thirty times as governor of the colony, told about the landing of the Pilgrims in his diary.

These were his words: "Being thus arrived at safe harbor and brought safe to land, they fell upon their knees and blessed the God of Heaven who had brought them over the vast and furious ocean, and delivered them from all the perils thereof, again to set their feet on the firm and stable earth, their proper element."

Leader:

What did the Pilgrims do after they landed?

Participant:

They soon decided the best place for their colony would be across the bay in Plymouth. The new settlers lived aboard their ship, going ashore to look for food and to cut down trees so they could build their homes. They also prepared land so they could grow crops when the warmer weather came. But now it grew cold.

Bradford wrote this in his diary: "It was winter, and they that know the winters of that country know them to be sharp and violent. What could they see but a hideous and desolate wilderness, full of wild beasts and wild men. Summer being done, all things stand upon them with a weatherbeaten face and the whole country, full of woods and thickets, presented a wild and savage hue."

Only the hearty and healthy could survive these conditions. Half of the Pilgrims who had come to America died during that first winter in the New World.

Leader:

How did the Native Americans and the Pilgrims get along together?

Participant:

When they first came ashore, the Pilgrims did not know what to expect from the Native Americans. They were unlike any people the Pilgrims had ever seen. Their skin was reddish. Many painted their faces in various colors. They wore bird feathers in bands around their heads. Their long black hair shone with bear grease. Their clothes were made of deerskin. But the Pilgrims soon found that the Native Americans could be their friends.

Leader:

Were any of the Native Americans particularly helpful?

Participant:

Yes, one in particular. His name was Tisquantum but he became better known as Squanto. He was a member of the Pawtuxet tribe that lived at Plymouth. Several years before the Pilgrims landed, Squanto was kidnapped by Captain Thomas Hunt of a passing English ship. Squanto then was sold into slavery in Spain. Somehow he escaped and found his way to England. In 1619, he was taken back to America by Captain Thomas Dermer.

While he had been away, tragedy had struck his tribe. It had been completely wiped out by a plague in 1617. So Squanto was the only survivor of the Pawtuxet tribe.

Leader:

How did Squanto help the Pilgrims?

Participant:

Squanto could speak and understand English, so he was able to talk with the Pilgrims. He showed them where to catch the fish in the waters around Cape Cod. He taught them how to plant corn that was the main crop of his tribe and to plant beans and pumpkins. He told them to wait in the spring until the leaf of the oak tree was the size of a mouse's ear—then it would be the right time to put corn seeds in the ground. And Squanto told them to put two dead fish in each hole where they planted seed. That would make the soil richer and the plants stronger, he said. The Pilgrims followed his advice and found that Squanto was right.

Leader:

Were the other Native Americans friendly?

Participant:

One of the most powerful tribal leaders in all of New England was called Massasoit by the English. That was his title as chief of the Wampanoag tribe and the English called him by that name although his real name was Ousamekin that meant "yellow feather." Massasoit was able to talk with the Pilgrims by using Squanto as his interpreter, since Squanto knew both the language of Massasoit and the English of the Pilgrims. So the Native Americans and the Pilgrims discussed how they could all live in harmony.

Massasoit agreed to a treaty of peace with the Pilgrims. For the rest of his life, Massasoit made certain that the Native Americans stayed on good terms with their new neighbors.

Leader:

What happened to the Pilgrims after their first hard winter in America?

Participant:

The Mayflower that carried them across the ocean stayed in the harbor from when they landed in December until the next April. It then sailed back to England. The Pilgrims now were entirely on their own and knew their crops must be bountiful for their colony to survive.

Fortunately the weather in spring and summer was fine and the crops prospered. There was enough for the Pilgrims to put much of the crop in storage sheds so they would have food for the next winter.

Leader:

How did the Pilgrims celebrate their good fortune?

Participant:

Governor Bradford decided that the colony should hold a three-day feast and celebration— in his words: "that so we might after a special manner rejoice together." He sent four men into the fields to find game and fowl for the feast. The women kept busy for days shining the pewter pots. Everyone helped roast and bake food.

The governor invited Massasoit to join in the celebration. He urged the chief to bring some friends too. Massasoit came, along with ninety other Native Americans. For three days the Pilgrims and their guests feasted on wild turkey, geese and other fowl, corn bread and English bread, cranberries and various vegetables. Since the days were spent in feasting and games, it was a celebration and not a true thanksgiving in the eyes of the Pilgrims.

Leader:

Did the Pilgrims also hold what they considered a real Thanksgiving?

Participant:

Yes. In 1623, two years after the three-day feast, the Pilgrims held what has been called their "actual first declared Thanksgiving." They set the day aside to offer thanks when rains ended a long drought.

Over the years, the differences between the two events became blurred in the public mind. Now our observance of Thanksgiving Day mostly resembles the harvest celebration of 1621. What is important is that we are remembering brave people who faced the dangers of coming to a new world to be true to their beliefs.

25

Leader:

How did our American Thanksgiving become a tradition?

Participant:

As the New England area was settled, it became a custom for the people to rejoice after a successful harvest. They were following a tradition long observed in England. During our Revolutionary War, thanks were given for major victories. At the end of the war, George Washington set a day of thanksgiving to mark the return of peace. Our young nation observed national Thanksgivings in several years until 1815. Then the custom was discontinued for almost half a century.

Leader:

When did Thanksgiving become an annual national holiday?

Participant:

Our modern series of annual Thanksgivings began in 1863 and the persistence of Mrs. Sarah Josepha Hale was an important factor. She was editor of Godey's, the largest woman's magazine of its time. For forty years, Mrs. Hale had written to every President to urge that there be an annual national Thanksgiving Day. She said one reason was to honor the American woman since women would prepare the feast and preside over the dinner. Thanksgiving would also give Americans a chance to offer, she said—and these are her words—"a renewed pledge of love and loyalty to the Constitution of the United States, which guarantees peace, prosperity, progress and perpetuity to our Republic." In 1863, Mrs. Hale wrote to President Lincoln.

Leader:

What was Lincoln's reaction to her request?

Participant:

President Lincoln twice before had set national days of thanksgiving for Union successes during the troubled days of our Civil War. Mrs. Hale now asked the President to proclaim Thanksgiving as a national holiday unrelated to any specific event. Lincoln issued such a proclamation in October 1863, setting the day of observance as the fourth Thursday in November. Other Presidents after him made this a tradition. Many years later, in 1941, Congress voted to make Thanksgiving a national holiday that each year would be on the fourth Thursday in November.

Leader:

Now we know why we celebrate Thanksgiving today. With this knowledge—and being a little hungrier since it took a while to find out—let's all enjoy our Thanksgiving Dinner.

A Portfolio

of

"Thanksgiving Day" Prints

by Winslow Homer

Winslow Homer's "Thanksgiving Day" Prints

Probably the finest illustrations depicting the traditions of Thanksgiving Day are the woodcuts by Winslow Homer printed in Harper's Weekly in the early 1860s. They are reproduced here by permission of the Metropolitan Museum of Art.

As a New Englander by birth with his parents also from the region, Homer had a geographical headstart to be Thanksgiving's prime interpreter in art. John Wilmerding, in a biography of Homer, said he was "a quintessentially American artist. The forthrightness in both his character and painting reflects his deeply ingrained New England background."

Summing up the artist's work, Wilmerding wrote: "Homer's singular independence and self-reliance, his practicality and care, along with his celebration of youth, endurance and the out-of-doors, all seem to be distinctively American traits. Homer's art represents the culmination of that 19th Century reverence for the physical and moral forces of nature."

Homer was born at 25 Friend Street in Boston on February 24, 1836, to a mother who was a talented watercolorist from Maine and a father whose family over several generations had lived in Massachusetts. His father's losses in a venture related to the California Gold Rush made it impossible for young Winslow to go to college as his older brother had done. Instead he went to work in 1854 for the Bufford lithography business in Boston, which had about a hundred employees. Some of his early efforts showed a developing sense of humor, as in "Man on a Rocket," a pencil sketch from 1849 in the collection of the Museum of Fine Arts in Boston.

After a few years with Bufford, Homer decided to work for himself, setting up his own studio mostly for wood engraving. For the recently-started Harper's Weekly, he free-lanced sketches of such subjects as football matches at Harvard and ice-skating on a lake in New York's Central Park. In 1859 he moved to New York, maintaining a studio on Washington Square for many years.

When Lincoln visited the city on his way to Washington for his inaugural, Homer sketched him speaking from the Astor House balcony for Harper's and the magazine also used his drawings of the inauguration. Harper's sent Homer to the battlefront during the Civil War for several visits starting in the fall of 1861; two of his prints for the magazine, the first in 1862 and the second in 1864, depicting aspects of Thanksgiving at the front, are reproduced in this portfolio.

Although Homer's sketches appeared in Harper's through the mid-1870s, he had begun working also in oils in the early 1860s and some of his paintings were soon exhibited in Paris. His visit to England in 1881 initiated a period of paintings more heroic in subject and scope. He painted, often using vivid colors, fishermen and sailors in battles for survival with the sea off New England and in the Caribbean and other marine subjects, as well as children at play and rural scenes of the Adirondack Mountains in upstate New York.

Homer moved away from the New York art world and lived most of his last three decades quietly in Prouts Neck, Maine. He sought seclusion. He refused to cooperate with William Howe Downes, who had been helpful to him in the earlier stages of his career, when Downes set out to write a book on the artist. "It would probably kill me to have such a thing appear, and as the most interesting part of my life is of no concern to the public I must decline to give you any particulars in regard to it," Homer wrote. He died in Prouts Neck on September 29, 1910. Another biographer, Albert Ten Eyck Gardner, said of the artist: "Homer's way was always the hard, objective way of professional competence and personal independence."

Thanksgiving Day—Ways and Means
The Metropolitan Museum of Art, Harris Brisbane Dick Fund, 1936 [36.13.4(1)]

Thanksgiving Day—Arrival at the Old Home
The Metropolitan Museum of Art, Harris Brisbane Dick Fund [36.13.4(2)]

Thanksgiving Day—The Dinner
The Metropolitan Museum of Art, Harris Brisbane Dick Fund, 1936 [36.13.4(3)]

Thanksgiving Day—The Dance
The Metropolitan Museum of Art, Harris Brisbane Dick Fund, 1936 [36.13.4(4)]

Thanksgiving in Camp
The Metropolitan Museum of Art, Harris Brisbane Dick Fund, 1929 [29.88.3(6)]

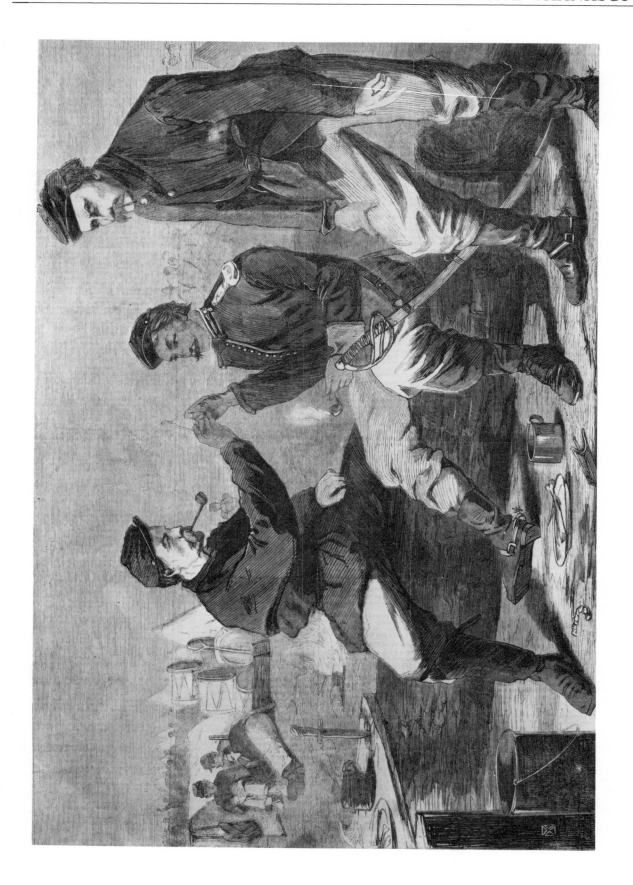

Thanksgiving Day in the Army—After Dinner—The Wish Bone
The Metropolitan Museum of Art, Harris Brisbane Dick Fund, 1929 [29.88.6(4)]

"I Never Knew *That* About Thanksgiving!"

It's an Old Custom

The custom of communal thanksgiving was practiced by the Canaanites of biblical times. During the Feast of Tabernacles, everyone lived in booths or tents in memory of the years when their nation had no settled home. The Book of Judges says: "And they went out into the field, and gathered their vineyards, and trode the grapes and held festival and went into the house of their god and did eat and drink."

In ancient Greece, a harvest festival, called the Thesmophoria, was a feast of Demeter, goddess of harvests. It was celebrated in Athens in November by the married women only. Their procession led to the temple of Demeter outside the city, where three days of thanksgiving were observed. The women then returned to Athens for a three-day festival.

The Romans held a festival of Ceres in October that worshipped their harvest deity. She was offered a sow and the first cuttings of the harvest. Music and sports were part of the festival.

Plutarch wrote of an emperor who returned to Rome after a disastrous campaign, concealed the facts and proclaimed a thanksgiving, which was duly celebrated. When the truth of the battle became known, the emperor said he didn't wish to deprive the people of a day of enjoyment.

The Mayflower Compact

The Pilgrims, in effect, landed where they were not charted to go, and this led to an agreement that set the standard for "government by consent of the governed" in America.

49

The Pilgrims' original destination was the area governed by the Virginia Company. Some of the Pilgrims believed, probably correctly, that they would not be welcome by the Virginians and wished to make landfall as far from Jamestown as possible. When the Mayflower dropped anchor in Cape Cod instead of a more southerly port, there was danger of mutiny by the non-Separatists and servants aboard who, in fact, outnumbered the Pilgrims.

The Pilgrims then drew up an agreement similar to covenants used by their churches. Signatories would be required to promise "all due submission and obedience" to the political body's "just and equall lawes." Almost all the adult males, including the non-Pilgrim settlers and servants, signed the agreement.

The Mayflower Compact set the precedent for similar agreements by the settlers of Connecticut, New Hampshire and Rhode Island. It was significant in establishing what became the American form of government that rested upon the consent of the governed. When the colonists elected Deacon John Carver their governor, he became the first governor in the New World chosen by free people in a free election.

The First Thanksgiving Menu

There are only two primary sources of information on the first Thanksgiving of the Pilgrims. These are reports of the day by William Bradford and Edward Winslow of the Pilgrim group. They do not include mention of the date of the observance, although it is known to have been between September 21 and November 9, 1621.

Based on the written reports, the Plimoth Plantation (see page 60) says that the feast included cod, sea bass, wildfowl (such as ducks, geese and swans), turkey, corn (and probably wheat) meal, and the five deer brought by Native Americans. James W. Baker, research librarian of the Plantation, notes that the term "vegetables" was not in use at that time and edible plants were known as sallet herbs, potherbs or roots. Herbs would be boiled with the meats as sauce or used in "sallets"— vegetable dishes either cooked or raw that could be a single vegetable or a mixture.

The Pilgrims regarded shellfish, plentiful around Plymouth, as poverty fare and thus not fit for a feast. Fruits would not have been in season but could have been dried by the Native Americans or preserved by the colonists. Beer and water, and possibly brandy, were the beverages. Goats may have been brought to Plymouth aboard the

Mayflower for milk but milk was not drunk whole and only occasionally as whey.

The Pilgrims had no molasses so they could not have served Indian pudding in its modern form. Baker also points out that cranberries might have been used in "puddings in the belly," what we call stuffings, but not in jelly or preserves because of the scarcity of sugar. Tea and coffee were not yet in use in England nor known to the Pilgrims, Baker says.

Meals were served at cloth-covered tables. Linen napkins were about three feet square since hands were used both to serve and to eat with. Trenchers or wooden plates took the place of dishes and two people sometimes would share one of these.

The Friendly Native Americans

The friendliness of the Native Americans in the Cape Cod area "singles them out from among all other tribes in the New World. It made enemies for them among their own kind," Henry C. Kittredge says in "Cape Cod: Its People and Their History." The writer, a descendant of the Cape's first settlers, adds that although some explanations have been offered, "why they were friendly is a mystery."

As for Squanto, he remained in Plymouth when Massasoit returned home after agreeing to the peace treaty with the Pilgrims. Kittredge says one reason may have been "because he fared better with the whites than with his own people." Bradford said Squanto, to the Pilgrims, was "a special instrument sent of God for their good beyond their expectation." Another said Squanto "wished to make himself great in the eyes of his countrymen" through his ties with the settlers.

Kittredge tells of one incident that dramatically demonstrated the Native Americans' friendliness. A troublesome Pilgrim boy, John Billington, became lost in the woods. "Less rigorous consciences than the Plymouth men's would have ascribed this happy accident to God's will and would have persuaded them that they were well rid of the young pest," but ten men guided by Squanto began a search. Billington was found by other Native Americans and brought by a large group of them to the search party. Kittredge suggests that the Native Americans easily could have killed the ten Pilgrims and thus reduced the number of able-bodied settlers by more than half. It "would probably have been a fatal blow" to the colony, "but the Englishmen, instead of getting arrows between their ribs or knives in the back, received food, water, information, guidance and presents."

... More About Squanto

One early account, not accepted by most historians now, held that the explorer George Weymouth took Squanto to England with him in 1605. This report also stated that Squanto stayed there several years, long enough to learn English well, and returned to America as an aide to John Smith. Smith was the Englishman best remembered for being spared, in Virginia, from death by Powhatan when Pocahontas, the chief's daughter, pleaded for his life. Smith had already lived quite an adventurous life, fighting against the Turks in wars in Transylvania and Hungary and being forced into slavery in Turkey, all before coming to America as a colonist. But Smith's life is another story, and an exciting one indeed.

There appears to be valid evidence that Thomas Hunt, a member of Smith's party, stayed on as a trader when Smith returned to England from America and that Hunt and his fellows seized Squanto along with 26 other Native Americans and sold them in the slave market at Malaga. Squanto was educated by Spanish friars and then managed to ship to London. He was attached to a merchant's family in England until 1619, when Captain Thomas Dermer took him aboard an expedition that returned Squanto to his old home.

Squanto's story ends sadly. In 1622, he was caught doubledealing and Massasoit sought his death. But in the same year he died of illness, "asking his friends," says one source, "to pray that their God admit him to the English heaven."

The First Presidential Proclamation

A speech in the new Congress on September 25, 1789, by Elias Budinot of New Jersey, led to the first proclamation of a Thanksgiving Day by a President. Budinot requested that a committee be formed to ask President Washington to set for all Americans "a day of public Thanksgiving and prayer, to be observed by acknowledging, with grateful hearts, the many signal favors of Almighty God, especially by affording them an opportunity peaceably to establish a Constitution of government for their safety and happiness."

Some in Congress objected to the proposal. Aedanus Burke of South Carolina said such an observance would "mimic European customs when they made a mere mockery of Thanksgiving."

Another South Carolinian, Thomas Tudor Tucker, asked: "Why should the President tell the people to do something they might not have a mind to do? How do we know the people are thankful for a Constitution that hasn't been tried out very long?" He said thanksgiving "is a religious matter, and as such it is proscribed to us."

The proposal won out, and Washington issued the first national Thanksgiving proclamation. He set the observance for Thursday, November 26, 1789, and prayed that day in New York City, the first seat of government for the Republic, at St. Paul's Chapel.

Washington's proclamation was lost as a public record for 122 years. It may have been misplaced by a member of the government among his own papers. It surfaced when the American Art Galleries in New York offered it for sale at auction, attributing ownership to a "private collection." The government retrieved the document with a purchase by the Library of Congress for $420.

Thanksgiving Day did not become an annual event, but Washington did proclaim a second such observance for February 19, 1795, this time on his own initiative.

... 47 Years With No Thanksgiving

John Adams, the nation's second President, was prompted by such concerns as "depredations on our commerce," which ultimately led to the War of 1812, to proclaim a national observance on May 9, 1798, for the purposes of "solemn humiliation, fasting and prayer," and thanksgiving to God.

His successor, Thomas Jefferson, believed that proclaiming a national day for thanksgiving was a "monarchical practice," and adhered to this conviction during his eight years in office. James Madison, in his two terms, restored the practice. Starting with the fifth President, James Monroe, none of the nation's chief executives for 47 years from Madison's last proclamation of April 13, 1815, opted for a thanksgiving observance.

The prayer day set by President James Buchanan in 1861 is not considered to be a national thanksgiving. With the nation troubled by the threat of civil war and high unemployment, Buchanan said he had been urged because of "the present distracted and dangerous condition of our country" to set aside a day for "humiliation, fasting and prayer throughout the union." He chose Friday, January 4, 1861, and asked "that the people assemble on that day, according to their several forms of worship, to keep it as a Solemn Fast."

. . . An 'Editress' Persuades a President

Sarah Josepha Hale is credited with playing a major role in President Lincoln's setting the precedent that made a national Thanksgiving Day a traditional annual observance. The New England states, during the period of no national observances, had generally continued the custom by their governors' edicts. Mrs. Hale was a native of New Hampshire, born there on October 24, 1788, so she was certain to have been influenced by her state's Thanksgiving Days.

Mrs. Hale had five small children when her husband died in 1822. She turned to literary work to support the family. Her novel, "Northwood; or Life North and South," included a chapter describing Thanksgiving Day on the hero's New England farm, in which the author noted her view that Thanksgiving Day "should be the same as the Fourth of July, a national holiday."

In 1828, she became editor of The Ladies' Magazine, published in Boston. Nine years later, the magazine was consolidated with Godey's Lady's Book, published in Philadelphia. Mrs. Hale became editor of Godey's, then the nation's largest-circulation periodical of any kind, and held the position for 40 years.

Each year in Godey's, Mrs. Hale wrote an editorial urging that Thanksgiving become a national holiday. She also wrote to state governors. Some recipients were hardly receptive, a conspicuous example being Governor Henry H. Wise of Virginia in 1856. He was a slave-owner and his answer—"this theatrical national claptrap of Thanksgiving has aided other causes"—represented mostly his view that it was a Yankee abolitionist holiday. All northern states observed the holiday at this time. Some Virginia cities in 1856 held their own Thanksgiving Day despite their governor's opposition.

Mrs. Hale also wrote letters to Presidents Fillmore, Pierce and Buchanan in her campaign. In 1863, after President Lincoln had proclaimed two earlier Thanksgivings for battlefield victories, she wrote him as "editress of The Lady's Book," asking "to have the day of our annual Thanksgiving made a National and fixed Union Festival." When he shortly thereafter proclaimed the holiday, Mrs. Hale wrote in Godey's that "President Lincoln recognized the truth of these ideas as soon as they were presented to him."

... The Civil War's Role

Both sides in the nation's Civil War observed Thanksgiving Days related to the battlefield. In September 1861, a proclamation by President Lincoln asked that Americans "pray for His Mercy; that we may be spared further punishment; that our arms may be blessed; and pray for the re-establishment of law, order and peace, and that the boon of civil and religious liberty, earned under His guidance and blessing, may be restored in all its original form."

In April 1862, Lincoln asked his countrymen for observances "at their next weekly assemblages in their accustomed places of public worship." He urged them "to render thanks to our Heavenly Father" with the hope that He might promote "restoration of peace, harmony and unity throughout our borders and hasten the establishment of fraternal relations among all countries of the earth."

After the Union victory at Gettysburg July 1-4, 1863, Lincoln set August 6 as a day for "humiliation and prayer," with the hope "that those in rebellion may not be utterly destroyed, but that they will lay down their arms and speedily return to their allegiance to the United States."

In the spirit of the New England tradition of Thanksgiving Days and thus setting the precedent for annual national observances since then and to this year, Lincoln's proclamation on October 3, 1863, invited his fellow citizens to "observe the last Thursday in November next as a day of thanksgiving and praise to our beneficent Father who dwelleth in the heavens." He reminded them of their blessings as the Civil War neared its end: "No human counsel hath devised, nor hath any mortal hand worked out these great things. They are the gracious gifts of the most high God, who, while dealing with us in anger for our sins, hath nevertheless remembered mercy."

By 1867, President Andrew Johnson was able to say in his Thanksgiving Day proclamation that he was adhering to "a recent custom that may now be regarded as established in National consent and approval."

... Immigration and Earthquakes

Thanksgiving Day proclamations often reflect significant events of the period or the temper of the times.

Ulysses Grant's statement in 1876, for example, made special note of the increase in migration from other countries to the United States.

He included among timely reasons for thankfulness that "His providence and guidance" had helped the government "to fulfill the purpose of its founders in offering an asylum to the people of every race, securing civil and religious liberty to all within its borders, and meting out to every individual alike justice and equality before the law."

Calvin Coolidge, in his 1923 proclamation, reminded Americans that they had been spared such tragedy as "the unparalleled disaster to the friendly people of Japan," the earthquake that took a toll of 200,000 lives.

When the clouds of severe economic depression began to darken the outlook a few years later, Herbert Hoover cited some silver linings in his proclamation. He noted "gains in the prevention of disease," along with his finding that "knowledge has multiplied and our lives are enriched with its application," while "childhood is measurably more secure."

Some Presidents found an outlet for lyrical expression in announcing the holiday. Chester A. Arthur said Thanksgiving Day was traditionally proclaimed "when the falling leaf admonishes us that the time of our sacred duty is at hand." Rutherford B. Hayes's statement begins: "The completed circle of summer and winter, seedtime and harvest, has brought us to the accustomed season at which a religious people celebrates with praise and thanksgiving the enduring mercy of Almighty God."

... The Roosevelt Ruckus

The most controversial of all Thanksgiving Day proclamations was Franklin D. Roosevelt's in 1939. The day he chose for the observance set off a furor that did not subside until Congress passed a law two years later taking the power out of the President's hands.

The nation was emerging from a great depression in Roosevelt's second term. Retailers became deeply concerned in 1939 about their business prospects when they noted that the last Thursday in November, the traditional day for the holiday, would fall on November 30. The Christmas shopping season is considered to run from Thanksgiving to Christmas Eve. The late Thanksgiving would leave only 20 shopping days for retailers to ring up sales in the year's principal shopping season. So their organization, the National Retail Dry Goods Association, petitioned Roosevelt to shift the holiday to the preceding Thursday, November 23. They also had asked for such action in 1933 when the calendar had presented the same problem but were turned down. This time Roosevelt acceded.

The nation erupted. Roosevelt's decision was front page news throughout the country. Public officials, churchmen and the general public sounded off. "Not for revelry and sport, and not for the inauguration of Christmas shopping, is this day set apart," declared Leverett Saltonstall, governor of Massachusetts. The Reverend Norman Vincent Peale told his congregation at the Marble Collegiate Church in New York that "the next thing we may expect Christmas to be shifted to May 1 to help the New York World's Fair of 1940." Cartoonists had a field day and editorial writers joined in the attack.

Many high schools and colleges were particularly upset by the President's move. Thanksgiving Day games were the traditional climax of many of their football seasons. The shift in dates meant their games would be played on an ordinary weekday rather than on a holiday since other scheduled games would prevent a change. In a nation that takes its football seriously this was no small matter.

Gallup pollsters found that 62% of Americans opposed the President on the change in Thanksgiving date, with preferences strongly tied to party allegiance. Governors could legally determine whether their states would observe the holiday on November 23 or 30. The result was a tie, 23 celebrating the earlier date, 23 the later date. Residents of Texas and Colorado had the good fortune of having two Thanksgiving Days that year.

In his 1941 proclamation, Roosevelt returned Thanksgiving to its traditional date. But Congress wasn't taking any chances. It took time out from the serious concerns of the nation—it had just been plunged into World War II—to pass in late December 1941 a Public Law establishing the fourth Thursday in November as the official date for Thanksgiving.

. . . *Proclamations Reflect World Affairs*

Harry Truman, who succeeded Roosevelt in 1945, had as intense an interest in history as any President. Thus it was fitting that the historic origin of Thanksgiving was given a role when he set the 1949 observance. With him when he signed the proclamation were high school students from Plymouth who brought him a piece of Plymouth Rock and a scroll with the text of the original account of the Pilgrims' first Thanksgiving.

One of Truman's major accomplishments was to establish a policy of aiding nations such as Greece and Turkey when they were threatened by communist takeover. This became known as the Truman

Doctrine and it was the reason he said in his Thanksgiving proclamation, "We are thankful that our resources enable us to aid the peoples of other countries in the furtherance of economic well-being and security."

Truman also sent American forces to South Korea in what was approved by the United Nations as a "police action" when that country was invaded by communist North Korea in 1950. Dwight Eisenhower, Truman's successor, was able to say in 1953 in his first Thanksgiving Day proclamation, "Especially are we grateful this year for the truce in battle-weary Korea, which gives to anxious men and women throughout the world the hope that there may be an enduring peace."

Eisenhower also urged Americans to bow before God "for wisdom in our striving for a better world."

... Views by Kennedy and Johnson

Although a native of Massachusetts, John Kennedy noted that Virginia also claimed a role in Thanksgiving history. "Over three centuries ago our forefathers in Virginia and in Massachusetts, far from home in a lonely wilderness, set aside a time for thanksgiving," he said in early November 1963 in proclaiming a holiday he would not live to celebrate.

Kennedy's spirit seems manifest in another section of his proclamation that also reflected the admission of Hawaii and Alaska to statehood four years earlier: "Today we are a nation of nearly 200 million souls, stretching from coast to coast, on into the Pacific and north toward the Arctic, a nation enjoying the fruits of an ever-expanding agriculture and industry and achieving standards of living unknown in previous history. We give our humble thanks for this. Yet as our power has grown, so has our peril. Today we give our thanks, most of all for the ideals of honor and faith we inherit from our forefathers—for the decency of purpose, steadfastness of reserve and strength of will, for the courage and humility, which they possessed and which we must seek every day to emulate."

Lyndon Johnson, taking office after Kennedy's assassination, urged that the fallen President's Thanksgiving proclamation be read, as a memorial to him, at church services on the holiday that followed the tragic event by only a few days. Many public observances were cancelled on Thanksgiving Day while others were held without the usual gaiety.

After winning on his own to serve the next term, President Johnson spotlighted key aspects of his "Great Society" domestic program in the first proclamation of his elected term. "In the past year we have added greatly to the national legacy," he declared. He said the nation had "guaranteed the right to vote to all our citizens. We have pledged dignity to our elderly—even in sickness. We have added new dimension to the education of our youth. We have broadened the horizons of opportunity for our poor." And he called on Americans to show "the courage—as shown by our sons in Vietnam today—to defend the cause of freedom wherever on earth it is threatened." The headlines on the day he issued his Thanksgiving message told of more American military personnel being added to the 160,000 already in Vietnam.

. . . Bringing the Record Up to Date

On the 1973 calendar, the fourth Thursday of November was the 22nd. That day would be the 10th anniversary of the Kennedy assassination. Some Americans felt it would be inappropriate to observe Thanksgiving on the anniversary of a tragedy. This sentiment was shared by some in Congress who believed the holiday should be observed a week later whenever it would otherwise fall on November 22. No action was ever taken for this purpose, but President Richard Nixon in his 1973 proclamation urged Americans to "pause to reflect on President Kennedy's contribution to the life of this nation we love so dearly."

President Gerald Ford's proclamation in 1976 was issued while the nation's celebration of its bicentennial four months earlier was still fresh in memory. "As we cross the threshold into our third century as a sovereign and independent nation, it is especially appropriate that we reaffirm our trust in Him and express our gratitude for the unity, freedom and renewed sense of national pride we enjoy today," Ford said. "Let us set a standard of honor, justice and charity against which all the years of our third century may be measured."

Another anniversary was marked by President Jimmy Carter in 1977. He noted that 200 years earlier, on learning of the American victory against the British at Saratoga, "Samuel Adams composed the first national Thanksgiving proclamation and the Continental Congress called upon the governor of every state to designate a day when all Americans could join together and express their gratitude for God's providence 'with united hearts.' " Carter's message said that "we have never lost sight of the principles upon which our nation was founded. For that reason, we can look to the future with hope and confidence."

Ronald Reagan's first Thanksgiving proclamation in 1981 stated that "Thanksgiving has become a day when Americans extend a helping hand to the less fortunate." His message continued: "Long before there was a government welfare program, this spirit of voluntary giving was ingrained in the American character. Americans have always understood that, truly, one must give in order to receive. This should be a day of giving as well as a day of thanks."

A Great Place to Visit on the Holiday

Not surprisingly, Thanksgiving Day is special where it all began.

Throngs of visitors join with local residents for the holiday activities in Plymouth, Massachusetts. The celebration starts with a mid-morning procession of townspeople who represent the Pilgrim men, women and children. The "Pilgrims" assemble "by the drum" and proceed to the First Parish Church in the center of town for non-denominational religious services. A public Thanksgiving Day dinner with traditional fare is sponsored by the Plymouth Area Chamber of Commerce; there are four sittings during the day.

Plymouth has much to offer visitors not only on Thanksgiving but year-round. The area has several historic houses which are open to the public. The Richard Sparrow House, built around 1640, is the oldest historic home in town open to the public and its clay-mortared fireplace is still used for occasional bread-baking and cooking. The Jabez Howland House, built in 1667, is the only house left standing in Plymouth where Pilgrims actually lived (the owner of the Sparrow House was not a Pilgrim); it has been restored and is furnished with many items typical of the period. The Harlow Old Fort House was built in 1677 with timbers from the Pilgrims' original fort.

A principal area feature is Plimoth Plantation, a "living museum" that re-creates the early settlement right down to guides' answering visitors' questions in the dialect of the day. Among the museum's attractions are Mayflower II, a full-scale reproduction of the type of ship which brought the Pilgrims to the New World. Another feature is the 1627 Pilgrim Village, where men and women are dressed in period attire and represent known residents of the colony. They discuss the homemaking, gardening, medicine, politics and economics of the period with visitors. The third principal exhibit of the Plantation is the Wampanoag Settlement, where visitors can learn about the culture, traditions and crafts of the Native Americans of southeastern New England.

Many other attractions add to the community's interest. Plymouth Rock, where the Pilgrims first stepped ashore in 1620, can be the starting point for a tour. Nearby is a wax museum, offering lifelike scenes depicting Pilgrim history while a collection of authentic artifacts from the period is at the Pilgrim Hall Museum. The Cranberry World Visitors Center has a multi-media show and exhibits on the history and culture of the berry. Tours and complimentary tastings are provided at Commonwealth Winery, New England's largest winery.

(An area guide is available free by writing Plymouth County Development Council, P.O. Box 1620, Pembroke, MA 02359, or by calling 617/826-3136.)

It's a Big Day in Virginia Too

Spanish explorers were known to offer thanks for safe passage when they landed on a previously undiscovered shore. So it's quite probable that the first thanksgiving in what is now the United States was in 1513. That's when Juan Ponce de Leon arrived on Florida's east coast on an exploration for Spain. In 1565, a thanksgiving ceremony was also held by Spanish settlers with local Native Americans in St. Augustine, Florida. Texas has a claim too for the first American thanksgiving, citing a service held by Francisco Vasquez de Coronado, a Spanish gold-seeker headed north from Mexico City with a large group of followers and thankful to find water and food in the Panhandle's Palo Duro Canyon. But these events are not tied in any way to our Thanksgiving Day tradition.

Virginians, too, claim that the first American thanksgiving, certainly among those under English sponsors, was held in their state; any early observances there are also unrelated to today's holiday. Jamestown was to be the first permanent English settlement in America when a party sent out by the London Company arrived in 1607. The "starving time" of the 1609-10 winter reduced the settlement from nearly 500 to only about 60 survivors who offered thanks on the arrival of a supply ship from England. It is also known that the settlers of an area known as Berkeley Hundred were under instructions to observe "a day of thanksgiving to Almighty God" each year to commemorate the day of their arrival in the New World in 1619. The Virginia colony perished a few years later.

The Jamestown Festival Park, a museum depicting life in early Jamestown and among the Powhatan Native Americans, annually holds a four-day special event starting on Thanksgiving Day. The celebration is titled, "Foods and Feasts in 17th Century Virginia." Demonstrations of the period's food preparation are held in James Fort, a re-creation of the settlers' first home. A whole hog is butchered and portions made into sausage or preserved by salting. How the colonists processed vinegar pickles, sauerkraut and mead, a beverage made from honey, is also shown. Shipboard diet is the subject of discussions aboard the Susan Constant, a replica of the largest of the three ships which arrived in 1607. In addition, the museum conducts a three-session workshop on 17th Century open-hearth cookery. Instructors demonstrate the making of pottages, puddings, pies and preserves. (Additional information on the Festival Park, located just south of Williamsburg, can be obtained by calling 804/229-1607.)

Thanksgiving 150 Years Ago

How did New Englanders celebrate Thanksgiving Day in the 1830s? The answers are provided by festivities that run from the Saturday before Thanksgiving through the weekend after the holiday at Old Sturbridge Village, Sturbridge, Massachusetts. The Village is a year-round outdoor living-history museum where visitors encounter everyday life in a small New England town in the 1830s. Founded in 1946, the museum has more than 40 buildings on over 200 acres and attracts more than 500,000 people each year.

The Thanksgiving celebration at the Village is based on how the holiday was observed by townsfolk some 150 years ago. Activities begin with a competitive turkey shoot. Contestants aim at paper targets, substitutes for the live birds sometimes used in such events in the 1830s. Breads, pumpkin pies, cranberry sauce, Marlborough Pudding, mince pies and other dishes are prepared while guides discuss early American recipes and food preparation. Other activities are grinding corn, making cider and crushing herbs and spices, with visitors invited to participate. On Thanksgiving Day the Village re-creates an early American service with psalms, sermon and prayers culled from manuscripts of the period. (For details, write Old Sturbridge Village, 1 Old Sturbridge Village Road, Sturbridge, MA 01566-0200, or call 617/347-3362 through July 16, 1988; the number after that date is 508/347-3362.)

Happy Thanksgiving! Foods

Turkey: A Bird That's Been Around

Turkeys have been a traditional part of Thanksgiving Dinners in America since the first Thanksgiving feast on Cape Cod. It's hardly surprising that the turkey has been cast in this role since it's a native American bird.

Fossil remains indicate turkeys roamed the Americas ten million years ago. And there's archeological evidence that turkeys were domesticated by the Southwestern Native Americans as early as the birth of Christ. Christopher Columbus and later Hernando Cortes, the Spanish explorer and conqueror of Mexico, enjoyed turkey enough to take birds back to Europe. Turkeys were being raised in the 16th Century in Italy, France and England. Thus, the Pilgrims likely were familiar with the turkey before they arrived in the New World.

Benjamin Franklin proposed the turkey as the official United States bird and was disappointed when the bald eagle was chosen instead. Franklin wrote to his daughter about the eagle's "bad moral character." "The turkey is a much more respectable bird, and withal a true original native of America," he wrote her.

Turkeys hit the trail in the early American West in the same manner as cattle. "Turkey drives" moved them to where food was needed. One big drive was over the Sierras from California to the hungry miners in Carson City, Nevada. And bringing the turkey's place in American history to more recent times, astronauts Neil Armstrong and Edwin Aldrin feasted on roast turkey from foil packets at their first meal on the moon.

... Turkey Tales and Trivia

Want to call the turkey by its scientific name? The American wild turkey is Meleagris (its genus) gallopavo (its species).

Why is the bird called "turkey?" Columbus thought the land he discovered was connected to India, where peacocks are found in considerable number. And he believed turkeys were a type of peacock (they're really a type of pheasant). So he named them tuka, which is peacock in the Tamil language of India. That's one explanation. Another claims that firkee was the Native American name for the bird. Or did the name come from the bird's call of alarm? It sounds like "turc, turc, turc."

Domesticated turkeys can't fly but wild ones can. They've been clocked at up to 55 miles per hour for short distances . . . Turkey eggs are about twice as large as chicken eggs; they're pale creamy tan with brown speckles. They hatch in 28 days (chicken eggs take 21 days) . . . While other types of turkeys have colored feathers, commercial turkeys have been bred to have white feathers. Eliminating pigment from the feathers results in turkeys that have a clean-looking skin when they're plucked—it's more appealing to consumers . . . Raising a turkey to market weight usually takes 16 weeks for hens, 19 weeks for toms . . . Heaviest turkey ever raised? It's said to be the 75-pounder raised by Jerome Foods, a turkey-farming company, in 1967.

Cranberries: Native Americans

There's no evidence that cranberries were on the menu for the first Thanksgiving Day. But the thornless cranberry vine was growing thick over the low, semi-swampy areas of Cape Cod when the Pilgrims landed. And the Native Americans were eating the berries cooked and raw. They also mixed cranberries with wild venison and fat, pounded the mixture to a pulp and patted it into cakes that were set on rocks to bake in the sun. This made what they called pemmican, a favored Native American dish with high energy content for the cold winters.

The cranberry is said to be one of the few truly native American fruits. Its botanical name is Vaccinium macrocarpum. To the Native Americans in the Cape Cod area, the cranberry was "I-bimi," or "bitter berry." Several theories are offered for the berry's present name. Cranes feed on the berry, some point out. Others cite the vine's nodding pink blossoms with their long pistils; these resemble the heads of cranes—thus, "crane berry."

In addition to using the cranberry for food, the Native Americans found it helpful in a poultice for drawing venom from poisoned arrow wounds. The women dyed colorful blankets and rugs with cranberry juice.

The Native Americans gave cranberries as gifts to the Pilgrims. In England at the time of the Pilgrims, women often made preserves and stewed fruits so they readily learned to adapt cranberries for these uses. One popular dish was a conserve of cranberries and apples, sweetened with syrup from pumpkin pulp.

In 1677, the colonists shipped ten barrels of cranberries to King Charles II. These went along with samp (broken and boiled Indian corn) and 3,000 codfish in an effort to appease the king, who had been angered when the settlers coined their own currency, the Pine Tree Shilling.

. . . 'A Bog Is Forever'

The cranberry is native to an area that extends from Nova Scotia, Canada, to North Carolina and westward to Wisconsin. Massachusetts is the leading producer with about half the nation's crop. Cranberries were harvested only from wild vines for nearly 200 years after the Pilgrims landed.

Henry Hall of Dennis on Cape Cod is credited with being the first to cultivate cranberries. About 1816, he observed that cranberries grew larger and juicier where sand from the dunes blew over the vines. He transplanted some wild vines to such a location and his success started commercial culture that still applies the same basic finding. Cranberry culture began in New Jersey in 1835 and in Wisconsin in 1853. Oregon got into the act in 1885 when a native of Cape Cod moved West with vines from the Cape.

Cranberry fields are called bogs but the berries don't grow in water. Plantations are built on peat swamps. They are drained of all water and a layer of sand about three inches deep is added to the rich peat soil before vine cuttings are planted. It takes up to five years for the first harvest, but some bogs have been producing for more than 100 years. "A bog is forever once it's planted," a grower says.

Sorting good berries from the bad is done today by the same principle used by the early settlers. They would set up a series of 10 to 30 steps. Good, firm berries bounced to the bottom like rubber balls; damaged berries are soft so they would stay on the steps. A mechanism that forces good berries to bounce over a small barrier onto a moving conveyer belt is used in modern processing.

Pumpkin: Another Native American

"Pumpkin pies, baked in large, square pans, were the first culinary Thanksgiving tradition," even preceding the turkey in its association with the holiday, Diana Karter Appelbaum writes in her comprehensive, carefully-researched volume, "Thanksgiving: An American Holiday, An American History." The tradition, however, could not have started with the first Pilgrim observance since, as she notes, the settlers had neither molasses nor flour for making the pies. Plain boiled pumpkins were used then.

Pumpkins, along with other squashes, belong to the curcubit family that includes watermelons, cucumbers, muskmelons and gourds. The United States Department of Agriculture says that "pumpkins and squashes are undoubtedly of American origin." Exploration of an archaeological site at the Ocampo Caves, Tamaulipas, Mexico, yielded seeds and a rind fragment in levels dated at from 7000 to 5500 B.C. Pumpkin fragments recovered from cliff dweller ruins in southwestern United States were determined to be from the basket makers whose civilization antedated even that of the cliff dwellers. Historical evidence indicates that pumpkins and squash were distributed along the eastern seaboard and throughout the Mid-West in pre-Columbian times.

How did the pumpkin get its name? The Department of Agriculture gives this explanation: "The name appears to come from the Greek 'pepon' or 'large melon' by way of the French which converts the word 'pepon' to 'popon' and then in nasalized form to 'pompon.' This eventually became 'pumpion' and the ending was converted to 'kin' in the American colonies and became 'pumpkin.'" A small, apple-shaped type of pumpkin now represented by the Perfect Gem was likely the first to be introduced into Europe, possibly in the 16th Century. A "gross watery pumpion" is mentioned in Shakespeare's "Merry Wives of Windsor."

The pumpkin has its place in literature and legends. The ghost in Washington Irving's "The Legend of Sleepy Hollow" lifts his pumpkin head from the pommel of his saddle and hurls it at the fleeing Ichabod Crane. Oversized pumpkins served as a golden coach for Cinderella and as the place of confinement for Peter the pumpkin eater's wandering wife. The pumpkin plant is a fast grower (a University of Missouri faculty member reported a vine attaining over-all growth of 1,986 feet in 173 days) but none can match the legend noted in The New York Times in 1963 of "a youth named Jack who mounted his horse on a spring day to plant pumpkins. Although he spurred his mount to top speed and dropped the seed in previously prepared hills he was unable to keep ahead of the fast-growing vines."

Help for the Cook

Preparing the Turkey

The following is based on information from the National Turkey Federation —

How much turkey to buy:

As a rule of thumb, plan one pound per person for turkeys under 16 pounds; ¾-pound per person for turkeys 16 pounds and over. These amounts should allay any fear of running short and provide some extra for next-day encores.

How to roast a whole turkey:

It's best, of course, to follow instructions that come with the turkey. If there are no directions:
Preheat oven to 325 degrees Fahrenheit. Remove plastic wrap. Remove giblets from turkey cavity and neck area. Rinse turkey well and pat dry with paper towels. Season or stuff turkey cavity if desired. Return legs to the metal "hock-lock" (the clasp that holds the legs together) or tuck under band of skin under the tail. Tuck wing tips under back of turkey. Place the turkey, breast side up, on a rack in a roasting pan. Brush with melted margarine or oil if desired. Make a tent of aluminum foil, shiny side in, and loosely

cover the whole turkey to prevent over-browning. Use this time chart for approximate roasting times:

Weight (lbs)	Unstuffed (hrs)	Stuffed (hrs)
4-6 (breasts)	1½ to 2¼	Not applicable
6-8 (whole)	2¼ to 3¼	3 to 3½
8-12 (whole)	3 to 4	3½ to 4½
12-16 (whole)	3½ to 4½	4½ to 5½
16-20 (whole)	4 to 5	5½ to 6½
20-24 (whole)	4½ to 5½	6½ to 7
24-28 (whole)	5 to 6½	7 to 8½

The turkey may be basted with pan drippings or other basting mixtures during cooking. Remove foil for the last 1½ hours of cooking to allow turkey to brown. Allow turkey to stand 15-20 minutes before carving.

How to check for doneness of a whole turkey:

Use a thermometer or pop-up timer. The point of the thermometer should be placed, not touching the bone, in the thickest part of the inside thigh when cooking a whole turkey, or in the thickest part of the breast meat when cooking a whole or half breast. The turkey should be removed from the oven when the thermometer registers 180-185 degrees in the thigh or 170 degrees in the breast. Let the turkey stand for 15-20 minutes before carving. This allows for the redistribution of juices and creates a juicier bird. The pop-up timer is set to pop up when the turkey is fully cooked.

Alternative ways to check for doneness:

A whole turkey is done if the leg joint moves freely when the drumstick is wiggled, or when a long-tined fork is inserted into the deepest part of the leg joint, the area is pressed, and the juices which run out are clear.

What you should know about frozen turkeys:

Scientifically, there's no difference in eating quality or flavor between fresh and frozen turkeys. The major difference: Frozen turkeys will keep for almost a year; fresh turkeys should be used three or four days after purchase. How to thaw a turkey: Place the wrapped turkey on a tray and thaw in the refrigerator, allowing five hours per pound of turkey. For quicker thaw: Immerse the wrapped turkey in cold water. Allow one-half hour per pound and change water frequently. Or place the turkey under a slow flow of cool running water and turn it often.

To roast a whole frozen turkey without defrosting it:

Use the same method as for roasting an unfrozen turkey except: a) Neck and giblets should be removed from the turkey. Do this as soon as the drumsticks can be freed to dislodge the giblet packet from the body cavity. Normally this may be done after two hours of roasting; b) Wing tips will remain in the natural position; c) Cooking times will be much longer. Use this table as a guide:

Weight (pounds)	Cooking time (hours)
12 to 16	4¼ to 6¼
16 to 20	7½ to 8½
20 to 24	8 to 9⅓

Procedure for stuffing a turkey:

Don't stuff the turkey until it's time to start roasting. When roasting a stuffed turkey, be sure to check that the stuffing in the deepest part of the turkey's cavity has reached a temperature of 165 degrees Fahrenheit before taking the turkey from the oven . . . Stuffing should be taken out of the turkey cavity before storing the uneaten part in the refrigerator.

***An alternative to baking a stuffed bird: Make a stuffing using broth made from the turkey's giblets. Then bake the stuffing in a greased casserole or securely covered pan for 30-60 minutes, depending upon the shape of the container and the oven temperature.

How to make broth from giblets:

Rinse and place giblets in a saucepan, add water, chopped onions, carrots and celery. Bring to a boil and simmer for at least 1½ hours. Herbs and spices such as bay leaf, peppercorns or ground pepper, parsley stems and cloves may be added for flavor.

Most common mistakes in preparing a whole turkey:

1) Over-cooking. Many people want to leave the bird in the oven even after the thermometer shows the turkey is done to be sure it's fully cooked. This usually causes the breast to dry out.

2) Failing to loosely cover the turkey with foil during most of the roasting time. This causes over-browning.

3) Stuffing the turkey the night before roasting or not removing the stuffing from the bird after roasting before it is stored in the refrigerator.

4) Forgetting to let the turkey set before carving.

What you should know about "sell by" or "use by" dates on a fresh turkey label:

A fresh turkey that has been properly refrigerated will maintain optimal quality for up to two days after the "sell by" date. On the other hand, a fresh turkey should be cooked on or before a "use by" date . . . If a fresh turkey has neither date indication, cook it within two days of purchase.

On storing a turkey in the refrigerator:

It's best to cook a turkey as soon as it has been completely defrosted—within 24 hours from the frozen state. Fresh turkey, like other fresh meat and poultry, is highly perishable. After purchase, the turkey should be refrigerated at 40 degrees Fahrenheit or below. It helps maintain quality if the sealed plastic bag used for fresh turkeys remains unbroken.

More helpful information on turkeys:

Overnight roasting is not recommended because turkeys should be roasted at a temperature no lower than 325 degrees Fahrenheit . . . Roasting turkey in a brown paper bag is not recommended since many bags are recycled and may contain chemicals which could be released in the cooking process. However, commercial roasting bags can be used. . . . It is not advisable to interrupt the roasting of a whole turkey by roasting it partly the day before and completing the roasting just before the meal. Partially cooked meat and stuffing are ideal media for bacteria growth . . . Basting ingredients in self-basting turkeys usually consist of vegetable oils, butter, seasonings, salt and flavorings. They enhance the tenderness of the white meat by keeping moisture in the white meat muscle cells.

(Help on any question related to cooking a turkey can be obtained free by calling 1-800-323-4848. It's the Butterball Turkey Talk-line, sponsored by Swift-Eckrich, the marketer of Butterball turkeys.)

Recipes for the Thanksgiving Dinner and After

Stuffing Ideas

Ham and Apricot Savory
Here's something wild and wonderful to add zest to your bird.

Ingredients:

Ingredients	Method
2 tablespoons butter 2 stalks celery, thinly sliced 1 clove garlic, chopped fine 1 medium onion, chopped	Saute lightly in butter in large skillet
2 cups day-old breadcrumbs (French bread or dry homestyle) 3 tablespoons chopped parsley ½ teaspoon mixture of thyme, marjoram, rosemary, sage or poultry seasoning 1 beaten egg	Toss together
⅓ cup dried apricots, pre-soaked and chopped 1 pound boiled ham, cut in julienne strips	Sprinkle both with 2 tablespoons brandy, then add to above mixture and toss well in skillet for about 3 minutes

Have fun—create your own special stuffing: Get in the spirit of the Chinese restaurant menu and its "one from column A and one from column B" by mixing and matching items from these different categories—
Bread:
      Sourdough/wholewheat/French/Italian/homestyle/cornbread/
      multi-grain
Or
Rice:
      Long-grain/brown/wild or basmati
And choose a few from the following:
      Celery/onion/mushrooms/green or red peppers/parsley/
      chestnuts/giblets/turkey or chicken liver/cranberry/watercress/
      black olives/walnuts/pecans/almonds/bulk sausage meat and
      apple/Italian fennel sausage/weiswurst (herbed veal)/sauteed
      oysters/spinach/bacon/carrots
Herbs:
      Sage/thyme/nutmeg/cinnamon/marjoram/herbs de Provence/
      rosemary/tarragon, or ready-mixed poultry seasoning

Accompaniments to Main Dish

Orange Glazed Sweet Potatoes. This spice-scented dish is fresher tasting than candied sweet potatoes, thanks to the special tang of oranges instead of calorie-laden butter and sugar. (Serves 6; multiply ingredients proportionately to serve more)

4 medium sweet potatoes
1 teaspoon grated fresh orange peel
½ cup fresh orange juice
½ tablespoon cornstarch
1 stick cinnamon
6 whole cloves

Rinse sweet potatoes with cold water and pat dry with paper towels. Prick each with fork, place in a shallow baking pan and bake in 400-degree-F oven 40 to 50 minutes until soft. Cool slightly; peel and cut into quarters. Thoroughly combine juice and cornstarch in saucepan. Heat on medium, stirring constantly until thickened. Add cinnamon, cloves and sweet potatoes. Turn down heat to low; cover. Simmer 15 minutes until heated through, stirring occasionally. Remove cinnamon and cloves.

Carrots Newburg (Serves 6)

4 cups diced uncooked carrots
1-inch boiling water
1 teaspoon salt
½ teaspoon sugar
2 tablespoons butter or margarine
2 tablespoons flour
¾ cup chicken stock
¼ cup heavy cream
½ teaspoon chopped parsley
¾ teaspoon finely chopped onion
2 teaspoons finely chopped green pepper
¼ teaspoon salt

Place carrots, 1-inch boiling water and 1 teaspoon salt and sugar in a saucepan. Cover and cook 12 minutes or until just crisp-tender. Melt butter or margarine in a saucepan. Blend in flour. Add chicken stock, cream, parsley, onion and green pepper and salt. Stir and cook 5 minutes or until of medium thickness. Add carrots. Serve hot.

3-Vegetable Saute (Serves 6)

1 pound snow peas (remove strings and ends)
½ pound mushrooms, cut in quarters
2 sweet red peppers, cleaned and cut into ¼-inch strips
1½ tablespoons olive oil

Saute mushrooms in ½ tablespoon olive oil for 5 minutes, turning often. Remove from pan. Saute peppers for 3 minutes. Cover and cook over low heat for 3 minutes; remove and set aside. Dry pan thoroughly. Heat 1 tablespoon olive oil and saute snow peas, turning often over high heat for 2 to 3 minutes, adding seasoning of your choice, pepper and salt to taste. Return mushrooms and peppers, mix lightly and serve immediately.

Great Go-Withs

Grapefruit Vegetable Aspic (serves 6)

1¼ cups grapefruit juice
1 envelope unflavored gelatin
¼ cup sugar
2 tablespoons lemon juice
1 tablespoon cider vinegar
Few drops red pepper seasoning
1½ cups finely shredded red, green and Chinese cabbage (½ cup of each)
½ cup finely diced carrot
¼ cup chopped red or green pepper
½ cup plain yogurt mixed with 2 tablespoons finely chopped parsley

In large pot, pour juice and sprinkle with gelatin and sugar. Warm over medium heat, stirring until dissolved. Stir in lemon juice and vinegar. Chill until slightly thickened. Fold in remaining ingredients. Spoon into 6 individual molds. Chill until firm. Unmold onto lettuce leaves and serve with yogurt.

Poached Cranberries (about 1 quart)

1 package (12 ounces) fresh or frozen cranberries
2 cups red wine
1 cup pure maple syrup

In heavy saucepan, combine all ingredients. Bring to a simmer over medium-low heat, stirring often. When cranberries start to pop, remove from heat; cool. Refrigerate 24 hours to mellow flavors. Warm cranberries just before serving.

Grand Finale

Cranberry Crisp (Serves 6)

3 cups fresh cranberries
½ cup granulated sugar
2½ tablespoons quick-cooking tapioca (or ¼ cup all-purpose flour)
Grated rind of 1 small lemon

Topping:
¾ cup all-purpose flour
¾ cup firmly packed dark brown sugar
¼ teaspoon salt
¼ teaspoon ground cinnamon
⅓ cup sweet butter, cut into small pieces
½ cup heavy cream, whipped to soft peaks

Preheat oven to 375-degrees-F. In bowl, gently toss cranberries, granulated sugar, tapioca and lemon rind until combined; spoon into 1-quart baking dish . . . To prepare topping: In bowl, mix flour, brown sugar, salt and cinnamon with fork or pastry blender. Cut in butter until mixture resembles coarse meal. Spoon topping over cranberry mixture; bake 20 to 30 minutes or until cranberries are soft and topping is crisp. Cool and serve with whipped cream.

Mincemeat Tartlets

1 package pie crust mix
1-pound jar prepared mincemeat (if desired, lightly sauteed apple chunks, and/or 1 tablespoon brandy may be added; stir well into mincemeat)

Prepare pie crust as per package instructions and put in refrigerator for ½ hour for easier handling. Roll out sheet and cut with fluted pastry cutter into rounds big enough to fit tartlet pans. Fill with mincemeat. Bake in moderate oven for about 10 minutes or until lightly browned. Cool in pan. Serve topped with whipped cream if desired.

Pumpkin Chiffon Pudding

Recipes for the traditional pumpkin pie may be found on the labels of leading brands of canned pumpkin. This recipe offers a lighter change-of-pace for your dinner.

1 16-ounce can solid pack pumpkin
1 cup half-and-half
3 eggs, separated
¾ cup sugar
Pinch of salt
½ teaspoon ginger extract
½ teaspoon nutmeg, freshly grated
½ teaspoon ground cinnamon
⅛ teaspoon ground cloves
(If available, add 2 tablespoons preserved ginger in syrup, chopped)

Preheat oven to 375-degrees-F. In large bowl, mix pumpkin, sugar, salt, cinnamon, nutmeg and cloves. Blend in beaten egg yolks mixed with ginger extract and half-and-half, and blend well . . . In separate bowl, beat egg whites until stiff and fold gently into pumpkin mixture. Pour into buttered 5-cup casserole and place on middle shelf of oven for 8-10 minutes. Reduce heat to 350 and bake for 25 minutes or until puffed and brown, and center is dry when toothpick is inserted, and pudding starts to pull away from side of dish. Place on rack to cool.

Holiday Encores

Forget the old term "left-overs." They're encores. These lively dishes can earn still more applause for Thanksgiving Day's turkey.

Easy Turkey Divan (serves 4)

1 pound cooked turkey meat
1 package (10 ounces) frozen broccoli spears, cooked
1 can (10-¾ ounces) condensed cream of mushroom soup
1 cup (4 ounces) shredded Swiss cheese
2 tablespoons dry sherry
⅛ teaspoon nutmeg

Cut turkey into ¼-inch slices; set aside. Place broccoli in 10x6x1½-inch baking dish; top with turkey. Combine soup, cheese, sherry and nutmeg in bowl; spread over turkey. Bake in 350-degree-F oven 30 to 40 minutes.

Turkey Pasta Primavera (serves 4)

1 pound cooked turkey meat
4 ounces spaghetti or fettucini
1 clove garlic, finely chopped
2 green onions, sliced
2 tablespoons vegetable oil
2 tablespoons water
1 pound fresh broccoli
1 cup (8 ounces) plain yogurt
1 teaspoon dried basil leaves
8 cherry tomatoes, cut in half
¼ cup grated Parmesan cheese

Cut turkey into ½-inch cubes; set aside. Cook pasta according to package directions. Meanwhile, cook garlic and onions with oil in large skillet on medium 3 minutes. Cut 1-inch flowerettes from broccoli; reserve remainder for another use. Add water, broccoli flowerettes and turkey to skillet. Bring to boil; turn down heat. Cover. Simmer 5 to 10 minutes or until broccoli is crisp-tender. Toss pasta with turkey mixture. Place on platter. Top with tomatoes. Combine yogurt and basil; spoon over pasta mixture. Sprinkle with cheese.

Turkey En Croute (serves 4)

1 pound cooked turkey meat, cut in small pieces
1 onion, chopped
1 red pepper, cleaned and cut in ½-inch strips
1 tablespoon butter
1 package frozen puff pastry— 2 sheets(thawed)
1 egg yolk

Sauce:
1¼ cups half-and-half
1 tablespoon cornstarch
¼ teaspoon dill weed
pinch of dried basil
pepper and salt to taste

Saute chopped onion and red pepper strips 5 minutes. Add turkey pieces. Cool. Reserve 1 tablespoon cold half-and-half and mix with 1 tablespoon cornstarch to smooth paste; set aside. Heat rest of half-and-half in skillet. Add paste and stir until smooth. Add seasonings and set sauce aside . . . Roll sheets to 14x11-inch rectangles; cut in half making 4 7x5½-inch rectangles. Place one-quarter turkey mixture on each and dribble 1½ tablespoons prepared sauce on each; fold over into a turnover and seal edges with water. Cut 3 1-inch slits on top of each to allow steam to escape. Brush tops with egg yolk beaten with 1 tablespoon cold water. Place in preheated 375-degree-F oven for 5 minutes; reduce heat to 350 for 20 minutes or until nicely browned. Before serving, heat sauce and pour small amount into slits and serve remaining sauce at table.